GW01017702

Playing wit Nursery Rhymes

Innovations by Ros Bayley & Friends

Illustrated by: Peter Scott

Produced by: Lynda Lawrence

Published by: Lawrence Educational
Unit 21, Brookvale Trading Estate,
Birmingham B6 7AQ

©   Lawrence Educational 2010

ISBN: 978-1-903670-83-5

CONTENTS

INTRODUCTION

The importance of children building up a repertoire of nursery rhymes cannot be overstated! Through enjoying nursery rhymes children acquire language, a sense of rhyme and generally develop the phonological awareness so necessary to later work in reading and writing.

However, once they have a basic repertoire of rhymes we can go so much further. By encouraging children to move from simply repeating the rhymes we have taught them to innovating and changing those rhymes we can develop vocabulary, creativity and imagination and thinking skills.

The rhymes in this book are all based on rhymes that most young children will have heard and learned throughout their time in early year's settings. There is no right or wrong way to use the book, simply introduce the children to the rhymes you think will appeal to them most and then use the suggestions included to get them thinking of their own innovations. Once you have done this you will probably find that they will begin to develop further innovations on rhymes that they may know, but are not featured in this book.

Ros Bayley

Little Green Frog
To the tune of *Skip to my Lou*

What you need: A soft toy frog or a small world frog.

What you do: Introduce the children to Little Green Frog and explain that they are going to make up a song about the day he went for a walk in the forest. Sing the new words (Below) Encourage them to join in.

Little Green Frog went for a walk

Little Green Frog went for a walk

Little Green Frog went for a walk

In the deep dark forest

Now lead the story on and make another verse by asking a question like, for example:

- Who do you think he saw?
- What do you think he saw?
- What did he do:
- What happened next?

Make up and sing as many verses as you like!

Find another character who might like to go for a walk in the Deep, dark forest.

I've Got a Mole Who's Stuck in a Hole

To the tune of:
What Shall We Do With The Drunken Sailor?

What you need: A soft toy or finger puppet mole and a length of plastic piping.

What you do: Place your mole character into the length of piping and explain to the children that he is stuck and cannot get out. Sing them the new words to the song. (Below) Encourage them to join in.

I've got a mole who's stuck in a hole
I've got a mole who's stuck in a hole
I've got a mole who's stuck in a hole
How shall we get him out?

Now ask the children for suggestions and then complete the song by using one of their ideas, for example:

We could push and we could pull him
We could push and we could pull him
We could push and we could pull him
To help him on his way!

Do this as many times as you like until the mole is out of the hole!

Thanks go to some great practitioners from Wakefield for this lovely idea

Would You Like To See the Mouse?

To the tune of *If You're Happy and You Know It!*

What you need: A mouse finger puppet.

What you do: Hide the little mouse in your hand and ask the children if they would like to see it. Sing the new words to the song. (Below) Encourage the children to join in.

If you want to see the mouse, say, 'we do!

If you want to see the mouse, say, 'we do!

If you want to see the mouse, come out of his house

If you want to see the mouse, say, 'we do!

Now, once you have sung the song let the little mouse pop out between your fingers. Then hide the mouse again and ask the children:

- What else could we do to get the mouse to come out?

Sing the song again using their ideas. Link several ideas together to encourage auditory memory, for example:

- If you want to see the mouse clap your hands, stamp your feet and shout, hello!

Teddy's Jumping

To the tune of *London's Burning*

What you need: A teddy bear, a selection of alternative soft toys and a set of action word cards.

What you do: Explain to the children that teddy has got rather fat from eating too much honey and needs some exercise. Sing the new words to the song. (Below) Encourage the children to join in.

Teddy's jumping, Teddy's jumping

Come and join him, come and join him

Jump, jump,   jump, jump

Keep on jumping, keep on jumping!

Now either:

- Invite one of the children to pick a card from the set of action words or to suggest a new way of moving. Repeat the song using the new action.

- Repeat the rhyme substituting different toys.

Pirate Patrick had a Galleon

To the tune of *Old MacDonald had a Farm*

What you need: Some small world toys around the theme of pirates.

What you do: Sing the new words to the song. (Below) Encourage the children to join in.

Pirate Patrick had a galleon, ee-eye, ee-eye, oh

And on the galleon he had a parrot ee-eye, ee-eye, oh

With a squawk, squawk here, and a squawk there

Here a squawk, there a squawk, everywhere a squawk squawk

Pirate Patrick had a galleon, ee-eye, ee-eye oh!

Now invite the children to:

- Choose something from the collection of toys around which to structure another verse.
- Suggest something else that Pirate Patrick might have had on his galleon.
- Suggest other characters that could be used for further innovations, for example, Spaceman Steven had a Spaceship or Mother Hubbard had a Cupboard.

Little Red Car

To the tune of *Bobbie Shaftoe*

What you need: A toy car

What you do: Sing the new words to the song. (Below) Encourage the children to join in.

Little Red Car rolled down the street

He did not know who he would meet

He stopped right by the traffic lights

Now who do you think he'll meet?

Now:

- Invite the children to suggest who Little Red Car might meet. Alternatively, let them select a character from a bag or box of things you have previously assembled.

- Ask the children to suggest where they think Little Red car may stop next, then sing the song again using their suggestion instead of the traffic lights

- Repeat as many times as is appropriate

- Change the type of vehicle in the song

Little Grey Squirrel

To the tune of *Here We Go Round the Mulberry Bush*

What you need: A squirrel finger puppet

What you do: Sing the new words to the song. (Below) Encourage the children to join in.

Little Grey Squirrel goes hunting for nuts

Hunting for nuts, hunting for nuts

Little Grey Squirrel goes hunting for nuts

In the enchanted forest

Now lead the story on and make another verse by asking a question like, for example:

- What do you think he found?

- Who do you think he saw?

- What do think happened next?

Continue until you have made as many verses as you want to.

The Fox is in the Box!

To the tune of *The Farmers in his Den*

What you need: A fox finger puppet or soft toy and a further selection of puppets or soft toys.

What you do: Place the toys in the box. Sing the new words to the song. (Below) Encourage the children to join in.

The fox is in the box, the fox is in the box,

E – I – N – G – O, the fox is in the box!

The fox has got some friends. The fox has got some friends.

E – I – N – G – O, the fox has got some friends!

Now:

Take one of the friends from the box but don't let the children see. Encourage them to ask questions to find out which friend you have taken out of the box. You will probably need to model this several times for them to get the idea. Have another adult ask you questions like:

- How many legs does it have?
- What colour is it?
- Where does it live?
- What does it like to eat? Etc. Repeat as desired.

One, Two, Three, Four, Five!

To the tune of: *One, Two, Three, Four Five,*
Once I Caught a Fish Alive

You don't need any props for this. Simply sing the new words to the children and encourage them to join in.

One, Two, Three, Four, Five

A swarm of bees flew in the hive

Six, seven, eight, nine, ten

Then they flew back out again

Why did they fly back out?

Because they heard the queen bee shout

'Come on boys we have to go,

Now hurry up and don't be slow!'

Now:

See if the children can, with your support, make up further innovations based on this rhyme. You could start them off by saying:

- One, two, three, four, five.
  Once I saw a duckling dive.

- One, two, three, four, five,
  I had a dream that I could drive.   Etc.

Nose, Knees, Tums and Bums

To the tune of *Heads, Shoulders Knees and Toes*

For this rhyme you will not require any props.

What you do: Sing the new words to the song. (Below) Encourage the children to join in.

Nose, knees, tums and bums, tums and bums

Nose, knees, tums and bums, tums and bums

And elbows and ankles and swing your hips

Blow a kiss with your lips, lips, lips.

Now:

- Encourage the children to think about how they could change the rhyme again by using different body parts and actions.

Don't worry if their ideas don't always rhyme. The important thing is that we accept the ideas they offer.

Brrmm, Brrmm, Little Car

To the tune of *Twinkle, Twinkle, Little Star*

For this rhyme you will not require any props.

What you do: Sing the new words to the song. (Below) Encourage the children to join in.

Brrmm, brrmm, little car

Travelling, travelling very far

Travelling, travelling down the street

 I work your pedals with my feet

Brrmm, brrmm little car,

Travelling, travelling very far.

Now:

Encourage the children to think about how they could change the rhyme again by using a different set of words. You may need to encourage them by asking questions such as:

- What could we have instead of a car?

Spiderman, Spiderman sat on the wall

To the tune of *Humpty Dumpty*

For this rhyme you will not require any props.

What you do: Sing the new words to the song. (Below) Encourage the children to join in.

Spiderman, Spiderman sat on the wall

Spun a web so he didn't fall

Along came Green Goblin who wanted to play

So they went to the park for the rest of the day.

Now:

Encourage the children to think about how they could change the rhyme again by using a different set of words. You may need to encourage them by asking questions such as:

- Who else might be sitting on the wall?

- What do you think they may be doing on the wall?

- Is anyone else on the wall with them?

Thanks go to practitioners in Huddersfield for this lovely innovation!

Miss Polly had a Trolley

To the tune of *Miss Polly had a Dolly*

For this rhyme you will not require any props.

What you do: Sing the new words to the song. (Below) Encourage the children to join in.

Miss Polly had a trolley that was stuck, stuck, stuck

So she called for the mechanic with his truck, truck, truck

The mechanic came with his tools in his hat

And he banged on the trolley with a rat-a-tat-tat!

He looked at Miss Polly and he shook his head

'You'll have to use another trolley.' he said.

'I'll take yours away to my house on the hill

And bring it back mended with the bill, bill, bill!'

Now:

See if the children can suggest other items belonging to Miss Polly that may need some attention, then, support them to write a new rhyme.

Thanks go to practitioners in Lewisham for this imaginative innovation.

Hippity, Hoppity, Hop!

To the tune of *Hickory Dickory Dock*

For this rhyme you will not require any props.

What you do: Sing the new words to the song. (Below) Encourage the children to join in.

Hippity, hoppity, hop

The frog sat on the rock

He jumped up high to catch a fly

Hippity, hoppity, hop

Now:

Encourage the children to think about how they could change the rhyme again by using a different set of words. You may need to encourage them by asking questions such as:

- What other animal could be in the rhyme?

- How might he move?

- What might he be doing?

Thanks go to practitioners in Birmingham for this lovely innovation!

Incy Wincy Spider Innovations

Try these innovations of this popular rhyme and then make up some more of your own!

Incy Wincy Spider met his friend one day

On a sunny afternoon in the month of May

They put on their sunhats as they went out to play

Holding hands together as they went on their way

Furry, furry, pussy cat climbing up a tree

A mouse ran down and so did he

He chased and he chased and he chased around the tree

Then they went off together to have a cup of tea!

Incy Wincy Spider sitting on my hand

Incy Wincy Spider now you're on dry land

You climbed up the water spout – got washed out by the rain

But now the rain has gone and you can climb right up again!

Five Little Ladybirds

To the Tune of *Five Little Speckled Frogs*

For this rhyme you will not require any props.

What you do: Sing the new words to the song. (Below) Encourage the children to join in.

Five Little Ladybirds sat on a window ledge

Eating the most delicious grubs, yum yum

One fell onto the ground where he was later found

Now there are only 4 little ladybirds – Oh no!

Etc, until there are no ladybirds left.

Now:

Encourage the children to think about how they could change the rhyme again by using a different set of words. You may need to encourage them by asking questions such as:

- What other animals could be in the rhyme?

- Where might they be sitting?

Thanks go to practitioners in Birmingham for this lovely innovation!

Drive, Drive, Drive Your Car

To the tune of *Row, Row, Row Your Boat*

For this rhyme you will not require any props.

What you do: Sing the new words to the song. (Below)
Encourage the children to join in.

Drive, drive, drive your car, quickly down the street
Pull up by the traffic lights,
Who do you think you'll meet?

I can see Spider man walking down the street
Off to catch the bad guys,
Who do you think he'll meet?

Drive, drive, drive your car, quickly down the street
Pull up by the traffic lights,
Who do you think you'll meet?

I can see Peppa Pig walking down the street
Jumping in the puddles,
Who do you think she'll meet?

Now:

Encourage the children to think about how they could
change the rhyme again by using a different set of
words.

*Thanks go to practitioners in Birmingham for this lovely
innovation!*

Roll, Roll, Roll in the Mud

To the tune of *Row, Row, Row Your Boat*

For this rhyme you will not require any props, although you might like to have the Three Little Pigs available as this rhyme is surely about them!

What you do: Sing the new words to the song. (Below) Encourage the children to join in.

Roll, roll, roll in the mud, merrily all day

If you see the big bad wolf, hide and run away!

Hide, hide, hide in the house, quietly all day

If you see the big bad wolf, scream and run away!

Drive, drive, drive your car, merrily all day

If you see the big bad wolf, honk and drive away!

Now:

Encourage the children to think about how they could change the rhyme again by using a different set of words.

Thanks go to practitioners in Birmingham for this lovely innovation!

Baa, Baa, Black Sheep Innovations

For this rhyme you will not require any props, although you might like to have some small world and superhero figures available to stimulate the children's imaginations for further rhymes.

Moo Cow, Moo Cow, have you any milk?

Yes sir, Yes Sir, as smooth as silk.

Some for the boy and some for the cat

And some for the children who are sitting on the mat

Bob the Builder, have you any bricks?

Yes I have and lots of sticks

One for Iggle Piggle and one for Fireman Sam

And one for Timmy the little Lamb

Now:

Encourage the children to think about how they could change the rhyme again by using a different set of words.

Thanks go to practitioners in Birmingham for this lovely innovation!

Squirrel Collects His Nuts

To the Tune of *Wind the Bobbin Up*

For this rhyme you will not require any props.

What you do: Sing the new words to the song. (Below) Encourage the children to join in.

Squirrel collects his nuts, Squirrel collects his nuts

Nibble, nibble, drop, drop, drop

Go and pick them up, go and pick them up

Run, run, quick, quick, quick

Point to the sky and point to the floor

Run around and find some more

Collect your nuts together one, two, three

Lots of nuts to eat for tea!

Now:

Encourage the children to think about how they could change the rhyme again by using a different set of words.

Thanks go to practitioners in Birmingham for this lovely innovation!